The Joy Luck Club:

The

Chinese American & Chinese-American

Ravyn Karasu

Ravyn Karasu

<u>ONE</u>

Thesis

In *The Joy Luck Club*, Amy Tan uses her personal experiences to share a world view of the novel's "liberated" Chinese immigrant mothers in comparison and contrast of tradition and liberation in their American-born daughters, showing the pride and struggles respectively of becoming a Chinese American and being born as a Chinese-American.

Introduction

In the novel, *The Joy Luck Club*, we follow the lives of multiple characters. These characters are described as "four women with different characters and their fates to immigrate to America when facing the dangerous disasters of the country" and their life and also covers the "growing experience of the four daughters of the four women" (Manjula and Govindaraj, 184). More specifically, four of these characters are Chinese immigrants that spend their lives struggling to balance their Chinese identities with their lives in America. The other four are the daughters of the immigrant women, born into American privilege as citizens and unwilling to accept their Chinese roots as part of their American identities. We are therefore privy to the lives of eight women and their struggles as immigrants and as the American children of immigrants. In the broad aspect of things, the story can be seen as an overall reflection of all the characters involved, as well as an attitude of survival and "finding that aspect of hope that allows a person to survive, be strong" and to deal with whatever it takes to accomplish that strength and survival (Essay UK). The novel presents the traditional Chinese beliefs and highlights the differences in the value of that heritage between the mothers and daughters (Manjula and Govindaraj, 184). The mothers bring this heritage with them in their safe space: The Joy Luck Club, where there is comradery in unfortunate pasts and within surviving in their new lives in America.

It is important to note that the novel comes from a place of familiarity and personal research. It then only makes sense that, to fully appreciate what *The Joy Luck Club* offers, we therefore must look to the author herself. As the novel goes on, coupled with information about Tan's family and experiences, we begin to see how the cultural struggles and personal identity of the characters is not their own, but also fit within the narrative that is Tan's own life.

<u>*TWO*</u>

Amy Tan & Her Characters

The Joy Luck Club is the debut novel of Amy Tan. She has managed to create believability by searching into her own past, experiences, and heritage so to lend a solid foundation to every character in some way. The more Tan shares with her public, the more we can appreciate her personal process and empathize with the positive and negative memories gifted to fictional characters that, in essence, may not be entirely fictional, but disguises for genuine experiences and the people in Tan's life (including herself) that are the ones experiencing them.

Amy Ruth Tan was born on February 19, 1952 in Oakland, California. Like the characters in her first novel, she was an American-born child of

Chinese immigrants. However, unlike her immigrant characters, her parents were illegal immigrants (PBS NewsHour, 1:23). Like the American-born daughters, Amy has both an American name, which is the name she uses for her writing career and personal identity, and a Chinese name that rarely has a use, but connects her with her Chinese roots (Tarintanir and Örürüm, 125). She even shared this name with one of the Chinese immigrant mothers in the novel: An-Mei.

Tan attended five different colleges and developed a fascination with language and spent a lot of time trying to learn about her heritage, often finding new information about her own family in the process. A lot of this discovery is present, not just in *The Joy Luck Club*, but all of her work henceforth. Tan states that, when it comes to her own creativity, "It [creativity] can come from an identity crisis: Who am I? Why am I this person" (TED, 2:53)? Though, she also adds "One of the principles of creativity is to have a little childhood trauma" (TED, 3:45).

Trauma is certainly something Tan experienced, especially in her young life. At the age of 15, both her brother and father passed away due to brain cancer, instigating a fear of a family curse in her superstitious mother. In an attempt to flee this curse, Tan's mother hurried with her to Europe where the two eventually settled for a while in Switzerland (Amy Tan Official Website). During this experience, Tan shares "When you are faced with the prospect of death very soon, you begin to think very much about everything. You become very creative, in a survival sense" (TED, 5:22).

Throughout her young life, Tan found communication with her mother confusing. Her mother would often give her strange anecdotes involving relationships and pregnancy. One such warning Tan remembers was "Don't' let a man/boy kiss you. You'll end up pregnant and you will kill the baby". Over time, she discovered "She [my mother] hid her past, but it always kind of snuck up in different warnings that she gave me" (PBS

NewsHour, 1:57). In due time, she learned that her mother's first marriage was to a sociopath and that she had children previously that she left in China, all of such information is presented by characters in *The Joy Luck Club*, via Suyuan leaving children in China and starting a new family in America, though a lot of Tan's mother is clearly present in the character of Ying-Ying. This connection is presented in Ying-Ying's strange tales and warnings given to her daughter, Lena. However, when *her* past is revealed, we learn that she was married to an abusive sociopath and Ying-Ying drowned her first-born son in her despair. It should also be noted that Tan meeting up with her Chinese half-sisters is also a major active plot point for Jing-Mei (Suyuan's daughter) in the novel. The experience, she admits, is what ultimately inspired *The Joy Luck Club* (Encyclopedia Brittanica). It's clear that "I look for personal meaning in my work" can be quite literal in Tan's creative process (TED, 7:39). "Past was always present in our lives," Tan says. "All these things from the past, they somehow rise up when you let go and say it's fiction" (PBS NewsHour, 2:23, 5:28).

THREE

The Woman & the Swan

Before the novel officially begins, we are met with a short story. It technically has no title, but we can give it the placeholder title of *The Woman & the Swan*. It's told in the manner of an old folk tale however it holds a lot of modern iconography and vocabulary. Therefore, it is ultimately a fake tale. It "overstates the misogyny of Chinese society. The implication of misappropriation is that Chinese-Americans—especially woman—are so assimilated that they have lost touch with their Chinese cultural origins" (Romagnolo, 92).

In short, the tale is of a woman of whom purchases a swan and brings it with her when she immigrates to America. When she arrives, the swan is confiscated from her and she is left with nothing by a few feathers. The whole time, the woman hopes for a better existence in America stating "In America I will have a daughter just like me. But over there nobody will say her worth is measured by the loudness of her husband's belch. Over there nobody will look down on her, because I will make her speak only perfect American English. And over there she will always be too full to swallow any sorrow! She will know my meaning, because I will give her this swan—a creature that became more than what was hoped for" (Tan, 2). There is a lot of great hope and disillusion in what the woman expects from America. It's clear the swan will represent all that she brings from China, something beautiful and glorious, which will be appreciated by her daughter. However, all the woman ends up with is one single feather. That is all that is left to share with her daughter after losing herself in the process of attempting to become an American. The woman, now old and looking at the lot she had received in her life, as an American, laments "…she had a daughter who grew up speaking only English and swallowing more Coca-Cola than sorrow. For a long time now, the woman had wanted to give her daughter the single swan feather and tell her '*This feather may look worthless, but it comes from afar and carries with it all my good intentions.*' And she waited, year after year, for the day she could tell her daughter this in perfect American English" (Tan, 2-3).

This short story full encompasses metaphorically everything that makes up *The Joy Luck Club*'s characters. The first part of the tale "implies an unproblematic transition between Chinese and American cultures;" and by its ending "the contradiction between an idealized version of assimilation to *American* subjectivity and the fragmentation of identity that historically marks immigrant experiences" (Romagnolo, 93). The idealized version of America and what it could offer to the immigrant mothers: An-Mei Hsu, Lindo Long, Ying-Ying (Betty) St. Clair, and Suyuan Woo is met with the reality that they must give up some of their

Chinese identity to exist as Chinese Americans. While the Joy Luck Club serves as a means for the four Chinese women to retain something of their heritage amongst each other, "a generational problem develops over time and cultural displacement occurs as family lives expand—it serves as a backdrop for the disorientation that occurs between generations" (Manjula and Govindaraj, 185). The four daughters: Waverly, Rose, Lena, and Jing-Mei (June) are disconnected entirely from their Chinese heritage, identifying only as Americans. They do not speak or understand much, if any, Chinese and cannot connect in any way, creating from these roots two separate identities between mothers and daughters. As far as the short story is concerned, the mothers are all the old woman wishing to gift something they treasure to daughters who see no value in that something, nor understand the purpose. The whole is gone and only a fragment remains. The daughters, for most of their lives, do not accept this *thing*, as, without the fullest context, it holds no value to them. As the old woman laments about wanting to instill the knowledge of her good intentions, she lacks the ability to do so. We see this in the way the mothers and daughters communicate, or more accurately, fail to communicate. Not only is there the language barrier, as the mothers *cannot* speak perfect English, but the meanings beneath their words also go misunderstood, adding another layer of language barrier between the two generations.

"In combining the contradictory impulses or desires (nativism vs assimilation), the symbol becomes unstable, unfixed, never to be resolved within Tan's myth… Furthermore, this symbol (the swan being torn away from the woman when she reached the United States) exposes the historical violence of immigration as well as the illusory nature of nativist and assimilist mythology" (Romagnolo, 94-95). Simply put, an important part of the Chinese identity the swan represents is removed to replace in it the Americanized identity generally forced upon immigrants when they arrive in the United States, as assimilation is how to survive in the country, with immigrants only grasping at what desperate little they can of their nativism to pass down their generations. This encompasses the entire narrative of the novel.

FOUR

The Mother-Daughter Relationship & American Experience

From the very beginning, we can see that the American experience is different between the four immigrant mothers and their four daughters. The daughters know nothing different than their American lives and the ease of assimilation from their peers. However, their mothers have spent their time in America trying to maintain their Chinese identity but also struggling to survive in America through assimilation. The struggles only continue when it comes to these mothers trying to raise their daughters with some sort of pride in the heritage and roots from which they come. From early on, we can discern that one culture is trying to dominate the other: both Chinese over American and American over Chinese (Priya).

Ravyn Karasu

Suyuan Woo makes a few good points in her experiences in China and America. When telling Jing-Mei about the original Joy Luck Club, she says "What was worse, we asked among ourselves, to sit and wait for our own deaths with proper somber faces? Or to choose our own happiness" (Tan, 12). Survival was definitely brutal in China for Suyuan, however we can see that the *new* Joy Luck Club serves a similar purpose among the new players. This is the place they can reflect on their lives and what it entails for them, rather than to despair alone. Suyuan and the other immigrant mothers were looking for something more in America. As the story begins, it is Jing-Mei that is taking her ignorant, American existence and seeking her roots after the passing of her mother. She's invited to take her mother's place and worries internally "How can I be my mother at Joy Luck" (Tan, 15). This cements one of the novel's themes. How can these daughters connect with their mothers and the mothers connect to their daughters?

Resistance from the daughters come from their very American outlook compared to the more traditional expectations of their mothers. The daughters seek their own freedom and independence while their mothers feel a need to govern their daughters' lives, as is customary of their Chinese culture (Priya). The daughters also have the privilege of understanding and speaking perfect English, and this privilege allows them the ability to *not* have to understand Chinese. Of course, this creates a rift between them and their mothers, the latter of which whom cannot speak more than broken English. This language barrier has made it impossible to communicate their feelings to one another (Priya). There is also a disintegration of old family structures in regard to Chinese traditions which becomes a constant conflict in raising their American daughters (Xu). Suyuan, in a sense, is the most like the woman in the *Woman and the Swan* tale in her idealist ideas of what America could offer her and her American-born daughter. Reality brought a hard blow to her expectations, and she is filled with a real possible fear: "She [Suyuan] has a fear that she will lose connection with her daughter, and that her experiences, thoughts, beliefs, and desires will have no future successors" (Xu). While the mothers and daughters do try to find some sort of reconciliation with one another throughout the story, it is Jing-Mei that seems to accept her Chinese identity the most in her search for connecting to her mother and her "Kweilin Story," a springboard to meeting her Chinese half-siblings and reuniting the two identities that Suyuan left behind in her passing.

The identities and lifestyles of the daughters are easily relatable as American, especially by those of us born into that American identity. It is true that they do have their own issues in their lives, both as children and as adults. It's important to the mothers for their daughters to accept their heritage, but it is a possible choice to remove themselves from this part of their identity. This is something that cannot truly be done by their mothers.

Like the *Woman and the Swan* tale, the mothers all escape to the United States in hope for lives that are much better than the ones they left behind in China. While a lot of misery is indeed left behind, the women are quickly thrust into the depressing reality of being an immigrant in *The Land of Opportunity*. Despite the adamant belief that anyone can be anything in America, the mothers find that the experiences they are forced into are less to satisfy their ambitions. In their cases, "survival comes first and with that, the women find menial jobs with long hours and poor pay" (Chen, 9). They were at the bottom and, when it came down to it, the women only had each other thanks to Suyuan's creation of the new Joy Luck Club. This proved to build for them a small community in which "no class or gender differences exist" and where these alienated characters could come together to be comforted (Chen, 23).

It is in their lives in China where the four mothers find *their* identity: who and what they are as people. They unlock a strength in them that they bring with them to America but maintain in a way their daughters are unable to understand. These women bring with them courage as they faced significant challenges while tenaciously seeking to change their fate from unfortunate to fortunate (Chen, 8). Of course, these fates eventually lead to a life of burden in America and a difficulty in raising their daughters in a place where these mothers are treated with little regard by others and, more tragically, by their daughters. If anything, the mothers come to realize that they cannot impose their understanding of their traditions onto their daughters, however they simply seek, in their old age, for their daughters to simply recognize and appreciate their Chinese heritage in addition to the American culture (Essay UK). Instead, their daughters feel not simply a disregard for these roots, but negative feelings towards their mothers on a personal level.

These girls do not respect their mothers and mistake their broken English and misunderstanding of American culture as a massive stupidity on the part of these women. They also feel a resentment to the pressures place on them to do great things and to be the object of pride for their mothers to show off. This is seen in both the cases of Waverly and Jing-Mei when it came to their talents. Jing-Mei was pushed to do all sorts of things, from piano to chess, in the hopes of being something like a "Chinese Shirly Temple" (Tan, 155). Unwilling to live up to these expectations, Jing-Mei has an outburst about not wanting to be a genius. As such, she is quickly corrected by her mother that the expectation was simply for Jing-Mei to do her best, not be a genius (Tan, 162-163). The pride of Lindo over Waverly also caused an act of rebellion, though in Waverly's case, despite her success, she simply stopped playing, an act that seemed less honest and more of a personal attack of spite on her mother. The issue is the language barrier that is created between the two generations, not just by linguistic vocabulary alone, but the way the language is used in their perspective cultures. However, the daughters are not the only ones creating this lack of understanding (in its entirety) between the two generations. The mother's certainly have their blame as well.

"All the mothers suffer the same problem: They do not want to talk about their pasts" and due to this, the concept of China and what their mothers endured to immigrate and bring them into existence is lost on their children, preventing the girls from obtaining any sort of wisdom (Manual and Govindaraj, 186). There is a cultural displacement from one generation to the next which serves as the backdrop of the family disorientation in the American setting.

While the girls, as adults, find a way to reconcile the rifts between their mothers and themselves, accepting something Chinese in themselves and still being American. For the mothers, each story they do not tell is tragic, but the actions of Jing-Mei become the symbolic and literal reconnection of past and present and the two separate cultures. She took Suyuan's *Kweilin Story* and, at the Joy Luck Club, faced the other mothers. This becomes a chance for them to attempt to open up about what they knew of Suyuan and offer her the means and support to go to China and meet her twin half-sisters. These siblings are a human representation of a world apart from the American life the girls take for granted. The twins offer a Chinese existence that is absolutely foreign to Jing-Mei and her peers, and she brings to them an American experience that is foreign to them. This union shows the conjoining of these two worlds and allows Jing-Mei to truly see herself as a Chinese-American and embrace her Chinese roots, the language, and the history that made up her pre-existence and eventually allowed her existence while she can pass on information about the mother her half-sisters couldn't get to know.

The mothers came from different places in their Chinese existence: Ying-Ying came from a rich family, but a bad marriage, Suyuan, the former wife of a soldier, became a refugee, Lindo was a clever girl escaping a loveless arranged marriage, and An-Mei survived the complicated family dynamic of her Chinese life. Once in America, these four women, alienated and isolated by their immigrant status and inability to assimilate as fluidly as expected, came together as one group to bring each other some sort of joy. The daughters, unable to comprehend or accept their Chinese heritage, went from this one place in their lives and went forth into their different places of existence as independent women with control of their socioeconomic status. The women have to accept their daughters' choices and lifestyles in their American identities, but there is still a clear hope that these girls would accept the Chinese roots into those identities, in essence, keep a part of their mothers and China with them.

FIVE

Conclusion

Amy Tan released *The Joy Luck Club* in 1989 as her debut novel. After this, she has gone on to write countless other pieces from novels to children's stories. In her novels, she is always somehow able to connect with the Chinese and American identities of her female characters. There is always something personal in her works that she pulls from a personal experience, not just from her familial experiences, but the immersion experiences of her research travels. She has devoted herself to understanding the experience of the Chinese, the Chinese American immigrant, and the life of a Chinese-American. As such, she creates characters with very believable experiences within her stories, due often to her fiction coming from anecdotes of real life to which she has been in some way exposed.

The Joy Luck Club effectively introduces us to Tan's understanding of the topic on which she writes, drawing from the experiences of her mother, grandmother, as well as the experience between her half-sisters and herself. The characters within the novel are all relatable and draw our empathy to their own unique situations. Unlike the two sides of the generation, we are privy to the dirty secrets and past events these women had to face as Chinese citizens. These are things their daughters cannot truly fathom, let alone simply understand and sympathize with the plight of their mothers. However, the traditional roots of the mothers make it hard to truly comprehend the identity of the all-American girl. However, we can relate to the frustration of the daughters trying to be their own people with mothers who want to govern over them the way their elders did to them. The strict structure isn't reinforced in the American setting and the mothers are left in their place as Chinese Americans and the frustrations that come with that, while their daughters deal with the ups and downs of being Chinese-American and the frustrations that come with that, as well. The Chinese American mothers have in them a wealth of knowledge and experience, and traumas that truly demand the admiration and sympathy of the reader, but that lacks from the daughters, of whom don't know any better. The Chinese-American daughters, on the other hand, have the opportunities that their mothers cannot achieve.

What becomes clear in these characters is the requirement of burden: Who has it? Can it be relieved? The Chinese-American daughters have the choice to accept their Chinese heritage. They will always be Chinese-Americans, whether they accept their heritage or not. They will always *look* Chinese, but they don't have to *be* Chinese. They have the ethnicity and the appearance, but otherwise, they can exist as American. It is the Chinese American mothers that have a heavier burden to carry. They cannot achieve anything that their daughters can achieve in America. They are Chinese. They cannot truly reject this identity, because it is who they are and that is the world that molded them into their adulthood. Their lives in America have left them unable to ever really master the English language and the American culture. They are *Chinese* American women who have Chinese-*American* children.

Works Cited

Chen, Yongjiang. *From Alienation to Connection: The Theme of Alienation Analyzed from a Socialist Feminist Perspective in Amy Tan's The Joy Luck Club*. 2014. School of Languages and Media Study, MA thesis. Hogskolan Dalarna,

Encyclopedia Brittanica. "Amy Tan." *Encyclopedia Britannica*, 2019, www.britannica.com/biography/Amy-Tan. Accessed 14 Apr. 2019.

Essay UK. "Essay: The Joy Luck Club." *Essay UK Free Essay Database*, 21 Mar. 2016, www.essay.uk.com/essays/english-literature/essay-the-joy-luck-club/. Accessed 14 Apr. 2019.

Manjula, M., and C. Govindaraj,. "The Challenges of Cultural Translation and the Problems of Immigrant Identity in Amy Tan's The Joy Luck Club." *Language in*

India, vol. 18, no. 12, Dec. 2018, pp. 184-
188, *SNHU Shapiro Library*. eds-a-
ebscohost-
com.ezproxy.snhu.edu/eds/pdfviewer/pd
fviewer?vid=0&sid=e094535d-6e0b-487b-
9eb9-09455c925e6c%40sdc-v-sessmgr03.

PBS NewsHour. "How Amy Tan's Family Stories
Made Her a Storyteller." *YouTube*,
14 Nov. 2017,
www.youtube.com/watch?v=HNGYAw_
3JQ0. Accessed 14 Apr. 2019.

Priya, Lakshima. "Cultural Barrier through
Communication - As Explained in Amy
Tan's The Joy Luck Club." *Language in
India*, vol. 12, no. 1, Jan. 2012, *SNHU
Shapiro Library*. eds-a-ebscohost-
com.ezproxy.snhu.edu/eds/detail/detail?v
id=0&sid=58dcca21-4946-472c-a69c-
5768c166de41%40sdc-v-
sessmgr04&bdata=JnNpdGU9ZWRzLWx

pdmUmc2NvcGU9c2l0ZQ%3d%3d#AN
=71958480&db=ufh.

Romagnolo, Catherine. "NARRATIVE
BEGINNINGS IN AMY TAN'S "THE
JOY LUCK CLUB": A FEMINIST
STUDY." *Studies in the Novel*, vol. 35,
no. 1, 2003, pp. 89-107, www-jstor-
org.ezproxy.snhu.edu/stable/pdf/2953355
0.pdf?refreqid=excelsior%3A55883575d41
917a6a8afcdfd26c7dbed. Accessed
14 Apr. 2019.

Tan, Amy. *The Joy Luck Club*. Kindle,
Penguin, 2019.

---. *Amy Tan Official Website*, 2017,
www.amytan.net/. Accessed 14 Apr. 2019.

TANRITANIR, Bülent C., and Gamze
ÖRÜRÜM. "STRUGGLE FOR AN
IDENTITY IN AMY TAN'S THE JOY
LUCK CLUB." *The Journal of International
Social Research*, vol. 10, no. 48, Feb. 2017,
pp. 1-6, *SNHU Shapiro Library*.

www.sosyalarastirmalar.com/cilt10/sayi48
_pdf/1dil_edebiyat/tanritanir_bulent.pdf.
Accessed 14 Apr. 2019.

TED. "Where Does Creativity Hide? | Amy
Tan." *YouTube*, 23 Apr. 2008,
www.youtube.com/watch?v=8D0pwe4va
Qo. Accessed 14 Apr. 2019.

Xu, Ben. "MEMORY AND THE ETHNIC
SELF: READING AMY TAN'S THE
JOY LUCK CLUB." *Melus*, vol. 19,
no. 1, 1994, *SNHU Shapiro Library*. eds-a-
ebscohost-
com.ezproxy.snhu.edu/eds/detail/detail?v
id=0&sid=403fe091-a99a-4b8d-baf3-
d1ba634eb54e%40sessionmgr4009&bdata
=JnNpdGU9ZWRzLWxpdmUmc2NvcG
U9c2l0ZQ%3d%3d#AN=edsjsr.10.2307.
467784&db=edsjsr. Accessed
14 Apr. 2019.